EVENTS & CELEBRATIONS

POEMS BY R. G. VLIET

NEW YORK : THE VIKING PRESS

First published in 1966 by The Viking Press, Inc.,
625 Madison Avenue, New York, N.Y. 10022.

Published simultaneously in Canada by
The Macmillan Company of Canada Limited.

The poem sequence "Clem Maverick" was published originally in *The Texas Quarterly*. The two prose poems first appeared in *Quarterly Review of Literature* ("The Journey") and *San Francisco Review Annual* ("The Ants"). The other poems, with two exceptions, were first published in: *Accent, The Beloit Poetry Journal, Epoch, The Hudson Review, Kayak, The Massachusetts Review, The Minnesota Review, Prairie Schooner, Quarterly Review of Literature, San Francisco Review, Saturday Review, Southwest Review, Stolen Paper Review,* and *The Transatlantic Review.*

The author is grateful to the sponsors and editors of these and other such magazines for the publication they provide.

Library of Congress catalog card number: 66-15877

M B G

Printed in U.S.A. by Vail-Ballou Press, Inc., Binghamton, N.Y.

FOR ANN
AND FOR ALAN DISTLER,
HARRY CLAUSS

If I walk through Texas
I will think of you . . .

CONTENTS

I

II

III

III (CONTINUED)

IV

V

NOTE:

In most of these poems, the title line is also the first line.

I

Poetry (if it must come)
must come never kept,
but unkempt and dragging weed
up from the seas, must be
bulbous-eyed from old
astonishments: a crank
species meant not actually
to be seen. Yet sweaty fishermen
hauling continually from need
sometimes fetch it up: it flops,
thumping the decks,
croaks—the fishermen
think they hear it speak.
More certainly it squeaks,
being slung in insubstantial air
and with all a dizzy ache
behind its gills. Its claws,
which must drip antique
moss, gesticulate: it knows
a city that is only deep below.

That sense as in the tragedies
one moves ultimately from hatreds
into cold stone: blood spills
in the end into the tall pillars,
the veined stone that holds
rages and fears, and shapes
them cold, the molten
not congealing, but—as if plunged
through smoky ice—snapped
brittle into stone: the tall
pillars one senses at the last
in the tragedies: Klytaimnestra's
tongue announcing
triumph like rocks that drop
and pile about her feet,
her body that was leonine
and strung with blood
now cold as a pillar, her thigh
granite. Become perpetual.

But such are the hates we hamper,
such the deceits and lies
that never come to murder,
that stay sheltered, never
come to horror, are never
transcended by act, such such all
the violences we harbor
with our half warm flesh, held
not to blaze but smoulder,
that rage simmers-down to a dry
pot and love diminishes in small
competition: we who are civil die.

The sun in one last high time
today wrenches the trees, streaks
the air with blue, with slowfires there.
Barbed fences of plumpowdered
blackberry hedge the year
and up in fields late hunters' blasts
clock the heart of the cock, weed
runner whose *cawk!* whose hot
blood jerks the winter seeds;
the world turns on its brittle stalk.

And that pale Lady shall ride down
from her hill tonight, white-lipped,
through blackened thistle and new blown
snow; the hurt cock shall tighten
beneath her breath o a frost is in her wrists
her hair is a twist of cold-cracked straw
and dry gourds rattle at her breasts;
and that stud her black steed
is nervous, nervous, and thick with seed.

As if *karew karew*
gulls beat up from mudflats
all the splotched islets
seeded rocks & flew

mad gulls gulls a clutter
of gulls & gulls' cries
& invaded the inland sky
the groundward flutter

of sparks pinfeathers
& fluff from collisions
karew karew a vision
of insane weather

overhead & hove down broke
branches in a pear tree
knocked cows to their knees
beneath & *karew* flocked

as they tried to rise
against their ribs pecked
ears udders & necks
irises from eyes

they bellowing & kicking
sobbing blood & cud juice
& cried *karew karew*
wings & beaks sticky,

as if all fish shrieked
in schools & finflash & scales
scraping & the crushed gills'
pink gasp & trekked

to estuaries dammed the rivers
on fishflesh made villagers upstream
fight floods & then swam
up to nibble them for dinners,

as if from the cuddling muck
seacrabs hoisted their limy
backs & weeded slimy
claws & scuttled up to stalk

spidery onto beaches & across
orchard & cornfield snipping
trees & farmers' legs & clipping
steeples & palps spreading froth—

so you my sailor man
who launched me as a minnow
from your thigh but will not
leave me free & I are come

to unnatural catastrophe
sink each other's ships cry
karew slam inland & slay
love which should pasture peacefully

as any spotted cow. I build
now of such pain & warped planking
as this craft shows to up-anchor
from where only rage is not killed.

Girls on saddleless horses
and wool scarving their cheeks
defy the glazed streets,
the wealthy heat of their bodies
(calyxed in sweaters and jackets)
thrives up from their horses
like forked slips and graftings,
the incontinent sap of their breaths
pokes stalks through the air—
such crunch and alarum of ice!
and under cramped elms
what a procession of greenery.

Games, hard press and bruise of the flesh,
boys banging one another, break and breathless
brush past arms, brash flagsnatcher!
push, press, pound, pummel and pop
bodies, hearts thick in the birdchests,
ache, squeeze, topple and tum-
ble tornshirted and kindercrazy, scramble and scratch
in the grass, bump bone and shoulder scratch,
smack, slap, swat, greenkneed, raw,
nosewhacked breath faster and cold,
shove! and then rip-out-ragged, knuckle, ankle,
stomach sucked tight on the run, balls
hugged up, trip, but though thump overhead
overheels, crumple safe at base, spit, rise,
spout snot and tearstreakers, bloodyhot rage,
rampage, weep, holler, clobber them, clout,
snort triumph! trample, gag, and rout:
not flags of sex even can brag such sport.

Three things you gave me,
three
things I shall not die: the burnt-
brown ample of your eyes,
a scar from childhood's risks
upon your cheek, your welcome me:
these are my flesh, those eyes
the dark I see most brightest by:
I am that child caught
in the skiprope, hit by the swing.
All doors, hands, lives you opened,
opening.
Two strange ships
crossed courses then, flashed
continents, made history of the sea.

Lady if you must walk that wood
beware of the dark chokecherry
of larkspur nightshade purple monkshood
palegilled toadstool and red baneberry

feed only on currants and ripe raspberries

crayfish from a brook. Watch a crow
doesn't peck your crumbtrail or magpies
snatch pebbles behind you as you go
and spiders crisscross mystery in your eyes.

Those woods thicken with each surmise

and if you should become lost Lady
do not at all push with your white
scratched hands against the night Lady

sit under a hemlock unsnarl your hair
hum ditties to whatever grizzly bear

do not at all weep do not at all shout:
I learned this once, and I think I've come out.

I pull you stalks of yarrow
white for your face. One night
and they'll tighten and yellow
but today I pull you stalks

of yarrow. I stick them everyplace
washtub, jam jars, in my hair
even. I don't know why
I pull you stalks of yarrow.

You fretted when we bought
this place the fields were choked
with the ragged white yarrow
(something strong and weedlike

in your face); you sweated over yarrow
forced wheat in its place
but it would crop up:
the fields are white again

today. And freshen how the loss
is. The smell of yarrow pinches.
The hairy stalks are rough,
untidier than lilies, real.

Robert it is eight months to the day
Farrel and you came last down to the pier:
there was rent to pay and Farrel's wage
and the debt on the *Kane*. But god I'd begged
you to at least admit there's more
in construction or trucking or in factory pay,
more cash nowadays in a grocer's
palm, and you were handy as most for
these. But always the same, and I hated it, answer—
I need a work that fits to my hand.

Nothing is but it fits to my hand.
Farming's good: beans corn squash
fit, or cabinetmaking: there's something
snug about a board. I've no green
thumb like my grandpa's, nor a carpenter's fine
rule of thumb though I might wish
it, but for sure there's a power of fish
in the Sound. And seeing me vexed past
nagging, you'd slap the kitchen table,
oysterknife scars in your hand's heel,
laugh and declare that I was just
a woman who *needs* the smell of fish
(drag drag your goddamn trawl
below your old *John Kane*,
gun the chrysler hoist the crane
unloosen all that slop of fluke
searobin and queer mud to the deck,
spike it all stinking into barrels
like the drunks who poke trash from the green,
ice down your sole, hose down,
flounder home and bed-me-down fishscale
codcraw searobin salty mackerel):
there's a *living* in ditchdigging! You got up:

Oh yes, a living, you said. I broke
that morning the handle off my coffee cup.
Eight months to the day that was ago.

There was a three day warning by radio,
but the tide was high, the wind low,
the ice already stowed. You said
you must go. In a quiet tantrum
I stood at the window and watched the *Kane*
crawl out past the farthest island.
Now I walk on the stones below the pier—
wind high, tide low. Robert, I stare
out at the bay and at the Sound beyond
the swollen hardhumping low tide
groundswells and wonder. Wonder.
Now I stoop down, pick up an oyster-
half in my hand, and in my hand
a piece of smooth smoky pebble,
and three small buttons of seaweed
(it's a living you'd say) in my hand
and here now a heavy barnacled
conch slung up from mudsuck and still
meaty inside with snail, and I hold
them all
          I hold them all in my hand.

Now for the 20th straight time today
we've argued this same petty way.
First it was trout: you claim they rise
for pleasure, I say for flies;
and thimbleberry: you called it wild
grape, as if grape ever flowered
with such a five-and-salmon-petaled show;
and next blackberry, christening it fieldrose
or some such. I swear you don't know
a damned thing hardly that grows.
Possums are porcupines, garters rattlers in your
eyes,
and this moment, making camp, what cries
darknesses about us are bears in droves
instead of mere crusthunting redsquirrel spies.
I swear you don't know—
o christ, you win, naming now love
to me, you win, it's better so.

Swung in chains of her own beauty
hands worked for rings too perfectly

she walks burdened with her worth
lugging the coins of handsome in her skirts.

How shall she move her ingot lips
free mineral talents in her hips

how lift her silver lovely eyes
square from such circles mathematics of surprise?

Lovely lady, who would punish you
so make you too much golden to be true?

Most sing in praise of loveliness:
I clank the iron of your distress.

Four Small Songs

I

Somewhere in the night
the lovers lie in their beds
and sometime at the height
of shrill desire thread
their clamoring flesh
with silence: words are death:
love mutes their breaths
somewhere in the night.

II

Be imperfect as the scallop's wings
as dip of finches in their half-flight
keep something for imagining
something for delight.

Move your hands as blind moles teach
wear some irregularity in your face
even your lapsed and mottled speech
allows for grace.

III

Boned as stems
of dandelions
to fashion flight
the gulls the gulls
o are bright
in the upper
ache of flight

Death crank
their necks
like market hens
bone will set
to bone again
Death pluck
and pluck
a beltline hand
feather shall lift
flesh again.

IV

One, two, three can go,
husband, wife, and shadow.

A cove salt swim
would taste of gull-cracked mussels
the crabshell rifted by crab disease
the boy who furtively took relief
at sand's edge, terns' excretions
the ironworks' sewerage. If we come down
to the shore before the moon is bright
we'll hear the lovers churning
in the sand like many darkened
seabeasts; watch where you step
or you step on antennae-hands shaking
above the sand, sea-tortured anemone.

Sweet is the night air. Listen
to the clam creature suck and tide
ticked pulses, waves that push
their condoms to the beach. These thrive
by the rich sea by the rich
ironworks. Morning and they're gone
on tides or clockings-in, leaving
great sand scrawls like words
and picking among the jellied condoms, birds.

How limiting your pulse is,
what a rhyme to disorder.
Do not think on that, no,
but count, count kisses
or we frost the works
of clocks, set yardsticks
snapping like wildfire, no
do not think on that, though
bark unsleeve as after
a long rot and all
trunks stand luminescent,
no, or your bone,
no, do not think on that:
we know the pearls of oysters
wind back to a bare itch
and mother of pearl be broken
into the electric broth
—but up in the mountains
in the Sangre de Cristos
once I saw a snowshoe hare
by sprinkling blood across snow
hold a burning white owl
to pulse and fan above it
like any bronze seagull
in a grip of fountains.

Although some of the external incidents in this poem are based upon the public actions and published statements of various figures in the country-music world, the characters depicted here have no relationship to actual persons; they are entirely of the author's imagination and without existence outside the covers of this book.

Clem Maverick

Thamus, are you there? When you reach Palodes,
take care to proclaim that the great god Pan is dead.

✣

It's great to be king in glory
Even tho you have to fall

—Hank Thompson, singing

I

Today in the capital it's Clem Maverick Day.
High-stepping white-crotched majorettes gambol.
Corps of twirlers prance away,
tails snapping in the sun like shrimp for gumbo,

and boots cut tall and skirts cut short.
The entire legislature's adjourned for the day
to watch the apple-kneed twirlers sport
as twenty-seven hand-picked schoolbands play

Dixie and Aggieland and El Gaucho March
and a twelfth-term senator isn't heard to say
I tell you it's enough to put starch
in a body's collar, all that stray—

Dixie and Aggieland and Semper Fidelis.
Today in the capital it's Clem Maverick Day,
the governor a-saddle, the queen in her trellis,
the thousand-gallon stetsons of paper maché,

the rose-wove floats of Texas-size guitars,
the cowgirl duchesses in bannered cars.
The whole damn crowd just a-stomps and roars,
and tonight there'll be a host of recording stars.

II

These hand-dyed fancybelts cowboy-tooled,
these beltbuckles pounded, turquoised and diamonded,
these sand-bellied roll-brimmed 7X beavers
with leather hatbands,
this ruby-horned saddle to ride his finger,
this silver fiddle for his lapel, these leather
ties, silk ties, windsors, gamblers, hand-painted
sequined four-in-hands,

these rainbow britches, these spangled blouses
with the pearl snaps, these tall-up and silver-toed,
hand-carved and fancy-foxed veal and sharkskin
cowboy boots,
these dove-gray, canary-yellow, rhinestoned and satin-
lined,
ranch-cut in Hollywood, cockleburr
and Texas rose, doeskin gabardine
hillbilly suits,

this flat-top guitar that stopped many a beer bottle
in honky tonks, and when he'd gone high-class
this big blonde nickel-plated and eight-stringed
electric—*everything here but his great*
blue yodel.

Please do not lean on the glass.

III

I rid on down to Kern's
with the devil in my head

I said I'd have my darlin
or leave her old folks dead
Lordy that sun. But now werent
that a turrible thang to do? In that song
I mean.
Mmmm-mmmm Mmmm-mmmm
and off her hand took five gold rings
bowee down dee
Come tonight there'll be a breeze
on the Plateau. It always does. I use
to could lay on my pillow of a night and pick
song ballets out of it, it goes so sweet
and mournful.
Mmmm-mmmm Mmmm-mmmm
Hand me them other snapbeans.
That's
his daddy you hear out there in the thicket.
I never seen such a big-veined man. Oh,
and when he comes in he talks so loud
from the weather. He's nigh eighty. He caint
barely straighten his fingers from the ax.
But he's always chopped cedar. A man's
got to live, aint he? I mean live.
Sometimes them cedar needles puts such
a sweetness acrost his neck. And I fix
him beans and red-eye gravy.
Onct that man
pulled a fiddle like dipping honey from a bee
tree. Now how could a lonesome gal
deny a one like that?
leaf by leaf the roses fall
drop by drop the wells run dry
That's a dwellin

song and ought to be dwelt on the long
notes.
            Looky that hawk in his stoop
up yonder. Aint that a wonder?
                                                I suppose
you want to hear about Clem. He give
us this place. Course this country aint worth
a damn exceptin to hold the world
together. And for cuttin scrub cedar.
But that cedar lasts. It lasts
like bone.
              Hold this basin a minute,
I got to shift some.
                                And I had eight
sons and Clem was one. He come way
late. He was so *wrinkled* when he come,
like on the neck of a sheared goat.
And I never did know what to make
of him. But it was Jimpsie was the frolic
one. Him and Cade. They was a pair.
And Buckle got tall enough to try
a horse. But no taller. And there was Lee
and little Rudy. How the sun use to turn
in that boy's tow hair. And Ransom
and Johnny.
                   All gone but them last
two now.
              A body stacks up his life
like roughbark cedar posts.
                                        —But so
many chicks about my skirts! So
many chicks.
                   And I had one

daughter onct. Name of Gussie.
I aint never lost her face. I tell you
it'll take the steers of Hell to drag her
from my breath. Her dear small breath
I kissed it; she was perfect of light
and gentleness. It was a Wednesday she
took sick. She turnt such shining
eyes and fever cheeks. She burnt
along her hair. Days and days. She fair
went like kindlin. Then got so strange
and peaceable, like settlin of ashes and past
her hurt. Wanted up from bed. She said,
Mama it's so *light*. And her pore daddy
helt her thin as sticks in his arms
and she said, Put on my bonnet. I put
the little fresh muslin bonnet
on her head. She werent but five. I said,
Gussie do you want to see God? Yes
Mama. Do you want to see Rudy? Yes . . .
Mama —O Jesus got up. Got up
from the grave. Pulled off them grave
clothes. Shaken off the girdles, taken
the napkins from his chin and laid
them in the grave.
in that shining land above

But it's Clem
you're intristed in. Onetime down the Nueces
we was after pecans. Clem climbed black branches
to give the tree a shake, but it come
a rotten branch. Clem's arm never
did set too right. It's how come

he helt his guitar so peculiar.
and now my song is over
I will sing to you no more

IV

His face was dark as Mexico
and gun blue was his hair
and he has cleared two acres of thorns
and one of prickly pear, pear
and one of prickly pear.

The wife she stood by the kitchen shade
the rancher he stood at the door
"I've no use for you to finish my lots
and you owe me for beans and more, more
you owe me for beans and more."

"Don't go today my husband dear
for to lay your pile of thorns
I dreamt I heard the cruelest song
from the dark side of the moon, moon
from the dark side of the moon."

She had not sat from the locking of her doors
to combing back her yellow hair
when who should she see at her own window
a-watching her across his guitar, guitar
a-watching her across his guitar?

She had not gone quite from the room
not quiteways down the stairs
when who should she see at the bottom of the steps
with catclaw and cedar in his hair, hair
with catclaw and cedar in his hair?

"What o what do you want with me?
What do you follow me for?"
and she mounted brisk and she took three coins
and she flung them to the floor, floor
she flung them to the floor.

Then he took out his long penknife
he was fairly up the stairs
and he knifed her until her own heart's blood
ran down her milk white knees, knees
ran down her milk white knees.

He has made across the yard
and across one stony acre
where greenly grows the liveoak tree
and sweetly sings the mocker, mocker
and sweetly sings the mocker.

He leaned his back against the oak
he moaned above his guitar
it was the highest hour of day
but the brush smoke it climbed higher, higher
the brush smoke it climbed higher.

He sung Mexicano till he heard at his back
the husband and five tall neighbors

and he rested there and he waited there
and sweetly sung the mocker, mocker
greenly grew the liveoak tree
and sweetly sung the mocker.

v

Sure I knowed Clem Maverick.
We growed up together. Come acrost
his first guitar hangin in a liveoak.
Him and me that night was hot
after ringtails. Thought we'd treed
a ringtail sure. What we treed
was a old flattop guitar. But that's
a long story: nothin a stranger'd
be intristed in.
Learnt his chords
off a old nigger sheepshearer name
of Freejo. Blackest nigger I ever
did see. But after work that nigger
had lightnin under his thumbnail. Fair
lit up a guitar. "Git away
fum me, boy. Git away fum me
wid dat ol wetback guitar." But Clem
dogged his tracks. I'd a-been scairt
my ownself. That nigger hadn't
but three lefthand fingers. You ever
notice how Clem helt his guitar
so queer? Well his three-fingered
chordin was a sight queerer.
Hell,

in them days all Clem and me
ever give a good goddamn for
was huntin and to pick a sweet guitar.

VI

At thirteen
stuck his flattop in a towsack
and turnt pro.
Set up this threepiece combo
with me and Leon to back
on banjo
and bullfiddle and we was mean,
man, mean—
ah ha San Antone you oughta seen
us go.

I sung
backseat and Clem would yodel
up a storm.
I tell you it got warm
when we pulled out the throttle.
Clem
Maverick and His Cowboy Kings.
Wingdings
and hoedowns, county fairs, auctionings,
barn

dances, rodeos,
medicine shows and forks in the road.
Clem couldn't

of told you a music note
from a cowtrack, but he was good.
Folks wrote
in letters. We was on the radio
at Del Rio.
That night Clem yodeled from his toes
up. Had to tote

him from the mike.
Then come the honkytonk years.
That's a place
to dance some and mainly to raise
a row. Try to hear your ears
in that ratrace.
And the crowd so allfired thick
a puredee stick
couldn't stir it. And then to pick
a bass

fiddle
in all that beer and ruckus?
But one high
old Saturday night we done "I
Got the Word," Clem's first famous
song. *Whoo-ee,*
they went hogwild in the middle—
Clem busted a window
going, but lit singing and a little
sky high.

VII

Blue who ooo what'll I do
money's all gone what'm I comin to
and call me lonesome your wranglin heart
blues baby blues since we been apart

ah odle lay-hée   dee-o-dle lay-hée
dee o-dle lee-dle lo-dle lay-hée heee hee
dee-odle lay-hée-hee   lay hée-hee
dee-odle lay-hée-hee   dee-lay héee

my head tall up my heart low down
sunalong baby gonna leave this town
catch me a catcherful of mockerbird song
baby maybe you got me all wrong

cause a Saturday Sunday ever night
gotta be where the lights are bright
sunalong lord I'm on my way
catchin the midnight turnin day

ah odle lay-hée   dee-o-dle lay-hée
dee o-dle lee-dle lo-dle lay-hée heee hee
dee-odle lay-hée-hee   lay hée-hee
dee-odle lay-hée-hee   dee-lay héee

VIII

Pan piping his oattunes. "Sunalong,"
"Sugarbabe," "Five Miles from Dallas,"

"When the Great Day Breaks." And Clem
was real country. Picked his guitar
with a cactus sticker; likely had ringtails
grinning in his hair. *I caint*
read a note except in my heart.
But he could sew a song together
with a red hot needle and a burning
thread. His headpiece was crammed with suchlike
ditties: used to fetch them to me
scribbled on tobacco-wrappers and envelopes.
And sing? Could sing skywide, noodle
a note, drag a moansome vowel
then hitch it in mid-note and crack
it across his tonsils—*I wu-under.*
Pan. O Pan. And ramble up
into a yodel all high yonder
like a scissortail swung on a wind
off cedar. He'd suck that word love
off the roof of his mouth, his guitar just
a-blinking. O Pan! And he really
meant it. It was the wild and the lonesome
and the hurt. Women loved it. Some
angel must have pinched his hillbilly nose
to make him sing so pure mournful.
Here was a real troubadour. And I inked
him a pact with TopNotch Music.
I lined him out on the rustic circuit.
It was what he wanted. But o
you Goatboy, horns hung
in the branches.
O you jukebox warbler.

IX

I recollect about twict a year
or so he use to haul into town
wearin one of them there silk
tablecloths on his neck. Drove
two creamcolored convertibles equipped
with I don't know what-all: sunshades
unbornt calf, white leather
upholstery—like he'd just hove
smack through some herd of milk
cows or other. And he kept
this Spanish mansion off the square.
White. I reckon you found it
easy enough. The kings of Egypt!
You'd a-thought he wore a crown
sure. Lordy, the kings of Egypt!
But we was talkin about the weather.
I tell you, if I ever see a blade
of grass again, I'll walk around it.

X

The fan mail?
The fan mail?
The women. Man
you got no
idea. They wrote.
Man they sent
photos. They went
hogwild. All

he had to do
was pick out
the goodlooking ones
fire 'em a note
and they'd hightail
I mean hightail
it down on the run
from Dallas or Nashville
or Portland or Denver.
He shouldn't of never
of died. Never.

XI

Once he came to the Palace.
I saved out of my lunch money
for it. And first LulaBelle
came on and she was funny

and the Westerly Trio but we
wanted Clem Maverick.
And when we heard his guitar
it got quiet quick.

His guitar played so sad
prettier than on the radio
and then he begun to sing
baby-o baby-o baby-o

and walked into the light:
I shivered between my knees.

It made you want to squeal
and kick your feet and squeeze

him like a little boy
he was so lonesome cute.
I got all his records.
I got a whole suit

of drawers full. Without
"Sugarbabe" and "Blue No More"
I couldn't stand to work
all day in this dimestore.

XII

When does hillbilly
                    get to be Country
Music, honey?
                When you can wear
a mink like this.
                  I know it's June.
They're nice to drape
                     across a chair.
I got lots more
                right upstairs.
Like I say
           Clem was always
sweet to me.
             All his lovesongs
was writ to me.
                We knowed

true love.
Maybe in a minute
we could go up
and looky them others.
My mink I mean
and maybe show
you all my purty
cowgirl dresses
I got up there?
You probably heard
I aimed to be
a singer once.
I went to see
Big D Stompede
and maybe audition
and Clem seen me.
He weren't but seventeen
myself just a mite
touch older.
We was hitched
next night.
That fixed me
as competition.
He wrapped my voice
in a dirty apron
and made damn sure
it stayed in the house.
Not really.
I'm only joking.
Honey if we
was to go upstairs
we might could see
some of Clem's things.
I keep 'em locked

up sacred.
Or maybe you'd like
to come set here.
You want to know
how-all Clem wrote.
He'd listen a minute
and then start picking.
He use to say
if he couldn't get it writ
in half an hour
he'd toss it away.
Sweetie this talking
curdles my throat.
Pretty please
just a dribble.
Not too much.
Clem weren't all
so great as they say.
If TopNotch Music
hadn't juiced 'em up
they wouldn't of been
a single hit.
Me and Misery
Me and Misery
that's how it went
the whole damn day.
And amiddle the night
to get stab awoke
by a morbid song
name of "Blackjack"—
mostly about
burning arms
and eyesocket smoke?
I bet you never

heard *that* on wax.
It come from there:
that cedar-panel room.
He'd set in there
starknaked on the floor
but for a pair
of cowboy boots
and all that hair
and ever light
switched on bright
head throwed back
eyes scrunched tight
slamming a beatup
Spanish guitar
and singing "Blackjack."
"Leave me be.
Leave me be.
They's a scab on the sun.
I got black crickets
chawin my back."
And sleep 'til noon.
I think his body
was turning to stone.
And then head out
on the Hamburger Tour—
Dallas Fairgrounds
San Francisco Cow Palace
Seattle, Toronto
those thimble-breasted bitches
climbing all over him
the whole damn way.
But all Clem's lovesongs
was writ to me.
All Clem's lovesongs

was writ to me!

O

get the hell

get the hell

GET THE HELL

OUT OF HERE!

XIII

And towards the last
already half on his bronc from whisky
his outfit splotched with sequins and sweat
they'd have him propped in the wings, the fiddler
covering with a fast

fill-in, and ready
him up and hand him out to the stomping
and whistling. He'd stare a minute at the mike
up to his knees in electric cords
and about as steady

as a wet calf
his rhinestones blinking, his guitar swinging
off some gulch, and finally pull back
stifflike and tell them to go to hell.
They'd just laugh.

And tell them
to go get their money back, he weren't
going to sing. And they'd clap. —And the steel
guitar whip out like a pistol shot
and snap him

up onto his silver
toes, rope him into a deadpan dance;
he'd jerk inside his gabardine, pop
along his backbone like somebody cracking
dry cockleburrs

and give a hitch
a shiver to shake the wind from his feathers
and would he pick! would he yodel!
longgone, buddy, his gullet full of wild
and cedarbark scratch

like he'd never been curried
below the knees—and his Cowboy Kings
coming in behind him like a Baptist
choir: the electric steel slamming
through the brush, lead

guitar pecking
in amongst the peppercorns, kicking
up a dust, the sweetgums high in the trees
the old bull fiddle down
in the backseat necking . . .

And they wouldn't let him quit.
It crowded your ears to hear them holler.
He'd try to flat out, his Spanish guitar
crying, picking over the ruins
but they wouldn't let him quit.

He was the whole
show. We'd have to ring down the curtain
and then scrape Clem off the boards and tote

the pieces backstage. *Christ, drown me*
in a blue hole

I've heard him say.
And once yell out *They use me!*
They use me! Jesus, shuck
it off, give me some light! burn
this scab away.

And the audience on the prod
out front. It got to the point where I
refused to follow Clem on a show.
Don't throw *me* to the wolves, I'd say.
I ain't iron-shod.

XIV

Don't tell me how it was, good buddy.
I played fairy godmama to him.
In my various roles of blowfly and hounddog
and cockleburr (to use his words), I
was always under his skin or on his tail
or in his hair, one. LulaBelle the prize
retriever. My job was to shoo Clem
off the bottle in time for the next show.
And he was prone to pack a playful pistol
back of his belt: my job was, when he
was done dusting out his hotel room,
to go in and settle up the costs
and see they didn't sue. I reckon I knew

Clem good as any. He poured ketchup
on everything he et. Yep, and one minute
be bawling like a baby at a purty sunset,
next minute up on his hocks rampaging,
stomping a wad of money into the floor.

Once in Los Angeles when he was blue
and dry and looking to get hisself soaked,
we kept him all afternoon in a car. We done
the sights and took him down Sunset Boulevard.
He tried hard to be cooperative. "Well,
let's sing," he said. We begun "When the Great
Day Breaks," which was his favorite hymn.
Of a sudden Clem let out this animal screech
and twisted and flung his head across my lap
like some knotted bony old broken fist.
He sobbed in my lap, "It's done broke!
It's done broke. And they *aint no light*."

Lordy, like the saying goes: Hillbillies
drive the longest cars, and wear the biggest diamonds
and the flashiest clothes, and the raggedest underwear.

XV

Met him in Salina, Kansas.
"Come on down to the coast with me.
I got a boat in Port Aransas.
I got *two* boats in Port Aransas."
I was packed in nothing flat,
ditched my classes at the University,
headed for Texas just like that

in his air-conditioned car. Outside
Ardmore, Oklahoma, once, we stopped
to watch some leggy colts alongside
the road. They leaned to their mothers' sides
and ran through the short windy grass.
It was the only time we stopped
other than for drinks and gas.

Below Waco we outdrove a twister
and a Texas Ranger, Clem singing, and he
said I had yellow hair like his sister.
I don't think he even had a sister.
Also we never got to the coast.
Ended up in a State Fish Hatchery
smack against a cypress and almost

out there swimming with the fish.
As it was we were up to our gills in liquor.
We counted the moons with beards of Spanish
moss snagged and tugging in the cypress
branches. The hood was littered with moonchunks.
About that time the plot got thicker:
Clem was chasing me around treetrunks.

One place I pressed to a tree tight
and I might have been cedar except I was giggling
and except a mockingbird was scattering its bright
different-colored pebbles right
above and one fell down on me.
Then I was scared as anything
but Clem caught me under the tree.

It was some hairy wrestling. Without
his stetson he was almost bald. He had
a dimple like a scar next his mouth. I caught
a taste of it. And it turned out
all he wanted was me to ride
on his back. Can you imagine? I fed
the bastard some grass and got astride

him and whipped him with a grassstem
through the night air. We didn't get far.
He fell asleep. The bronco Clem
at Churchill Downs. I left him
and Man o' War in the vodka pastures
and followed my clothes back to the car
to pick the damn moss and cedar

sticks from my hair. I don't know
what kind of footprints we left behind.
Then I waited until it began to grow
light and watched the scissortails plow
their breasts into the watertop
and flutter up new from the pond.
Clem Maverick was still asleep

naked in the wet grass and his
wiry body-hair strung with dew;
I got my things and caught a bus
home. There. That's all there is.
It's enough. Now you see why you're
hearing this by phone? And don't try to
contact me. I won't be here.

XVI

In April that year
when half the Panhandle
was freighting across the sky

and the sun a brown
smidgin there and our teeth
gritty and sinuses dripping

with spring in the air
he come sure-enough blue
on a cracked sidewalk in Waco.

In the hospital downtown
he sprung his tubes and siphons
and greened-up and died;

his blood was laced
with Old Crow and Seconal
and mescaline and they put it down

to a heart attack
at age 29. The last word
we think he said was: *August* . . .

but let's face it
it don't make sense. The nurses
cleared away the gear

and let him go back
to the brushcountry ranchtown
down on the Divide where they

raise pricker
bushes and mohair. The local
Chamber of Commerce rigged

him a floral
thingamajig of guitars and memory
pillows in front of the courthouse

and the crowd was thicker
than crickets to the funeral.
The Chuck Wagon Gang

led with a choral
job of "Beyond the Sunset."
It was going on the wind

and folks cried
and really cried when Tex Jones
sung "When the Great Day

Breaks." It looked
to be a wet Mardi gras.
Women fainted. Flashbulbs

lit and died
like Clem hisself. And I got
the word. Now they really

got him booked
up solid. Now they really
got him down on wax.

XVII

What more do you want from me? What
do you fling this palaver in my face
for? I tell you I did for Clem
what he wanted. I lined him out
on the rustic circuit. I inked him a pact
with TopNotch Music. But this was a boy
with dark in his fingers from the word Go.
That's how he played. Or maybe it was
he had something to give and instead
they took it. Is that my fault?
For christ sake should he have been
some thin ditty along
some fencerow? a piece of piping
under mountain laurel? thistle music
off in the brush or what might
dance on a rock by night if you
could prove it any by this knot of hair
snagged to bobwire? There sure
wouldn't have been no cash in that.

XVIII

We wore long black
stockings then
and here's
me.
And here's Clem
way in the back

row
like he was trying to hide
behind trees.
He looks
sort of rabbit eyed.
That's just like him.

I remember his carved
sloped
desk
fitted him best
for sleep and how his set
head looked froze
in a poke
of nine
o'clock
sun
and one black
finger
in the ink and how
I didn't like him then.
Until at recess once
some boys with pencils and sticks
were teasing a hummingbird
caught
in a web
beating
like a piece
of green
fire
like a satiny
daymoth thing. All
green
and red

and yellow
and Clem let it go.

Then it was different.

Clem taught me how
to whistle on a piece
of panic
grass
and I let him
copy out my lessons
and yes onetime at lunch
we split a whole
lard
bucket
full of green
wild
huisache
honey
he'd climbed a bluff for
down the Nueces
and were
were
were
we sick.
Now he's yonder
under
the rock squirrels.

Let's go
outside. But look. Even
then
it was something old

about him.
Let's go
out.
Supper's cooked. And Jim
ought to be up from the pens
directly.
We could wait
under that big
liveoak
and then all three walk back
to the house. But Clem never
hurt nobody but himself.
Watch
you don't
skid
on the acorns
when we get there.
It's been a high dry year.
Still and all the ground
is drenched with
acorns.
And we
might can see
some late
goldeneyes and maybe see
goldfinches in the brushpiles
there.

Jim and me
just bought
this ranch. We hope to do
right well. But for years
nobody's kept the place.
I mean not to *live*.

Oh,
      they'd lease the sections
for browse right enough
but that's all. There was some
trouble
            here
                  a long
while
         back. Yes that's
a mocker. He'll do
                              it over.
And look
               at those
                           acorns.
That liveoak puredee *thrives.*

XIX

Another minute and we're on the wind.
Soon as Ma's Real OldFashioned

gets in her licks and then one
more plug for cold Lone

Star. Here we go. This opener
ranchero's what I call a roper

      I hate to see

it throws your heart. And old Clem

warbles it like it was hurting him.

it end

A TopNotch platter. The other side's
the splinter-kicker. Since Clem died

so sudden

he's took off from the hillbilly division
gone Top Ten across the nation

sprouting on jukeboxes everywhere. Yessirree
if they could peg Clem's dirty laundry

Have a little

at 45 RPM and spin it
man there'd be a fortune in it.

fun

It's like a white-eyed horse turned loose
raring and rampaging and tearing across

tonight

the countryside and folks chunking coins
at it to hear it screech. So if anyone

tells you Clem's dead that's a crock.
Take it from this old disk jock.

XX

goodnight sweet prince

DEAR CLEM,

we got the word
by phone you've gone away
bound for Home on the Glory Train
to a Brighter Day.

Dallas is pretty far
from Him in His Judgments There.
The Big Boss of the Roundup likely
wanted you near.

Now you're in Hillbilly Heaven.
Oh what a star studded land.
You'll write for the greatest singers Clem.
The Angel Band.

You'll broadcast from the Holy Station.
You'll purely pick your guitar.
The Heavenly Music will make us look
to the Western Star.

So you'll sing again you see.
They'll do you Up Yonder in style.
Still and all we're glad you sung
our way awhile.

Rest in Peace. And may
your songs Clem Maverick
make *His* Topchart.

Sincerely,

WE

AT TOPNOTCH MUSIC

III

Evergreens deck the year
in black and darker green
on the hill. Crows tell
what they will with laughter
or coughs across the snow.
Ashes are on the roads.
It is the broken-hip time,
and stripped willows and ribbed
deer. Here in a row
this natural fenceline, chopped
back to black scepters
in cold ermine, or fingerless
amputations, time-charred,
unwrapped from cruelest white
and welted from wrist to wrist
with old barbedwire, leads
us where we go. And if one
wild stump jabs
a pliant antler at our hearts,
still we learn nothing,
nothing that we want to know.
O my dear kind, my dear
kind, what is there to know
except this starstorm snow
again? And that high on the hill
the mute stepping grouse
under the very name of death
print the crust and peck needles
and make small breath.

Wild Asparagus

Poem, history, monument of weed,
old featherless fernbones mounted
to starkness, but lately a punctured hare
hauled its breath past the year's
dry mouth and spilt you its red
salt seed. Then how your roots

softened to vigor, and knot and knob
and crown—such candle thrusts, such albino
fingers to prize upward the dark
summer, tap the stretched drumhead
of the hare's death; now your triumph
rears sexual and muscular, caught

with rabbit hairs, probing, poking,
tilting the carcass, spreading the ears,
squeaking up between stiff feet,
and I, I take what I need,
asparagus spears, asparagus spears,
green-tasting, stringy, sweet.

Now name the season blackberry
manyseeded purpler of beaks
and this morning wiry
crabgrass agatestemmed by frost,
next the cellar a cold
fireless salamander in the mold:
summer reckoning up the cost:

what the walnut loses
husks thumpt down to charry
smut and milkweed flosses
tossed tossed like sparks
spilt become ash,
in a garden unpicked squash
fierce as summer on the dark

vine rotting, such showy weeds
as thistle mullein chicory
going to wreck and seed
and what is there now to show
for this summer fallen but waste?
all thrown corrupted all displaced:
by love we lose. By loss we grow.

A Letter

Today of all days I want
you here. It is a morning sprawled
through haze: late flies fumble
in the dry grass, robins cross
in fives, walnuts fall and the green
sun splits to its black core.
I am like a scrubbed child
shining out on all sides; I wear
a burnished oakleaf at my levi collar.
We would wade uptrail, splashing
our feet through this leafy tide—flakes
of an old sun. A woodpecker signals
from its stump. Squirrels run
like writing on a branch; something ticks
in this dead tree trunk.
                                        I want
to talk of the soul, which we have worked
so hard for and which daily upon me
grows more tangible. It gathers
toward, and it is mortal . . .
                                                    My heart
pounds upward through mountain laurel
toward those roosts of the winter crow.
Listen! this fellow is scolding me
here. Grouse burst upward;
it is all a drumming. And on above,
something antlered crashes the brush.

We shall be crowned with our deaths.

In a Photograph by Brady

I had never known
the art of truth until now
when I met you breathing
through the stain on Brady's photograph.
And I had seen the sleek mounts
with four hooves spread
precisely upon the grass,
bell-buttoned general
squat athwart, and I
had seen the squared-capped
private in Napoleonic pose
gracing the granitizing eye
peering from within its tent,

but I had never known
until now the art of truth.
For while the three beside you
tower in sculpture heroically
carefully as in a child's game
of statues, you bend to the moment,
your worn back to Brady,
your fist in a caisson's mud,
your face forever from the future,
intent only on the present pain,
and so, because you never needed
the camera's eye, alive.
It is the immortality
of this photograph that it, like art,
gives truth and being to him

who is not grasping for them.

And your hands (with hair
at the wrists through which the veins
plunge) are the only quick hands
of all that shaped the torn
cornfields, your back
the only back still
with blood to lift broken cities.
Your body this moment sings
ache and scar beyond bone:
yours the only flesh
exists, breath yours alone.

Another Photograph

I

Backed by pasteboard and a warp of years
you seem a small girl proper to seminaries
you seem so straitly proportioned and your wrist
sustains so delicately the false fenceprop.

Our Dear Friend says: Hardly. You were big,
bigboned to follow behind an ox,
manly upon a horse, sheepfetcher, could heft
a rifle through the brush, girl the hounds
led, winter needlegrass and buffaloburrs
festering your skirt. Onetime you wore
a choker of red laurelbeans and acorns.

But now your skirt is stiff and formal
as leather, heavy with hips, this day
prodded from seminary: you are poised
as a lady: upheld in the stiff back, breasts
under white blouse spattered with Saturday
lace, a cameo like a seal at your neck.

II

What is real, this or that other
day outside this picture when you woke
the sister here beside me now
Goodmorning, went out to a sound
of hounds, to such circles of morning
light,
        and found your self there
caught halfway through the wire,

the rifle hugged with sudden fact
to let a blunt tongued bullet
through your breast, your mouth pressing
kisses of dirt;

when your mother
rocked you in halfcircles of her distress
under a liveoak and never spoke
and pinched ripe burrs from your dress?

III

Doves in season fall.
Helped by ringtails, black
persimmons fall; the call
of hounds drops ringtails:
October when red laurel
beans, acorns of liveoak
fall. And the world is real.

For Ramona McBryde Peebles and Lorita Gibbens McBryde

Woven is this boy
and he is a net for catching
things. His interlacing
nerves, green strands
yet undistended, are the close
clinging mesh sweeping
beneath each stone, seining
the leaves: woven is this boy.
But he had passed mushrooms
barely buttoned, unblazed
by turtles, and dewy runs
unrabbited (so anticipatory
the morning of yet lipsealed
spring); past oak, hickory,
beech; now at last to willow;
and here, the only whispering
love within these woods,
moved the brook that had burst
continually upon him
through a long late snow;
here dreamt that emerald
curtain-eyed encavered croak
that had so often leapt
into the captivity of his thought.
. . . Soft the hunter, till down
a grass sprout sight
he spies his sickening joy:
now! Nets! Nets!
Quivering their need!
But when the will to cast
most commanded, the coolness
of the pool congealed his blood,
and he was trickle entranced,
mesmerized by the cool

love breaths of the pool,
the glistening inverted dripping
roothair of willows, and the fragile
swelling frogthroat colder
and whiter than snow in its dancing.
He never knew why, when he
was most the net for flinging,
he had need to untouch
the stillness and backing away
go empty netted home,
so much disturbed by silence.

The crickets in their antique real world,
shrill ethiops of the grassblade-cry,
and dustdrenched beetles clicking, and rasp
of fans where tobacco-rich grasshoppers fly
(though caterpillars climb by furry hunches
in silence to the ravel day), and dry
cornstalk scrape, and crows scaring
upward like scattershot peppering the sky,
and grackles and grackles and grackles in bunches
breaking southward from their sparse branchberths
with a rinsing noise—the year's full
hull receding through highnoontide surf.

Love's own form
is sufficient unto
itself: never ask how or why:
purpose puffs a grape, is its purple hue,
packs apples; winged maples fly;
horses dogs deer run wordlessly
perfectly; the hand in love
moves through its own country:
love has no use for less than love:
love made these poems. I don't know why.

IV

The Journey

Beyond, beyond him, beyond his body and his father's house the ocean is whispering him awake, prepare. For it has risen finally above the night's low tides, swelling from the branched lime of coral, sneaking mutely across the reefs of his sleep (or had he even slept?), lifting those pools stranded in the lava rock (where outcast fish all night had quietly shrieked, sensing excommunication) and widening them into sea and him into morning and being.

Awake, prepare: into his smallest bone despite his watchful sleep the night has packed provision, blood rewound, brain secretly flexed on dream; and now the ocean is whispering at the edge of his bed where his fingers stir damply in the sweat of almost beginning. (But it is the impatient sea-breeze squeezing through the half-light, admonishing the palms, insulting a muffled dove, ordering the rockcrabs out for breakfish, and breathing onto him, tasting first and salty. And then it is his mother above him, breathing onto his eyes *awake; prepare.*)

He is suddenly today, this, and now! as his mother laughs, wringing her hands at her chin merrily, and as he swoops whoops naked into his shorts and tennis shoes and laughing to beat the sun.

(And from their lava pools the fish have been accepted.)

Already that plebeian spy his father has hurried to sanctuary in the house's temple and living room and before the great black plates and dials and knobs of distance is bowed, making morning ceremony, surreptitiously confessing to absent priests the political inclinations of the masses—ocean, wind, and sky: *Leone to Pago Pago. The night is done; no ships came through; we are here, we are up, we are waiting. Only the sun is half awake. The horses are waiting: they will take us to that village.*

And then breakfast is served (for him and the rockcrabs) and the sun tossed caviling out of sea and sent stumbling about the village to play mean morning tricks: catching mosquito nets down dawnwhite and naked, fooling a vain plain lizard into an orange chameleon, sprawling purposely onto a terrace of peaceable fiddlers to set them scuttling holeward—each last one shaking above the sand a claw outrageously caught on fire before drawing it down and snuffing it there—and at last settling self-vindicated in a ripe papaya.

Now his father has assumed his office of doctor and its kit: needles and tongue-sticks and sealed gauzes. Now his mother fixes blessing on his quick cheek and lunchsack—then out of the house and porch onto day as he laughs her good-by. *Good-by.* Good-by to the native nurses smiling there three in their dispensary blouses and red lavalavas (one is twisting her hair darkly in the teeth of a turtle comb, one pressing the nightseed from her eyes, one simply watching). Good-by to Sa'ii with whom he climbs trees. Where *he* is light and moving, light in his tennis shoes upon the broken coral path, Sa'ii stands with his brother drowsing onto his back, bent beneath his brother's sleep. *Good-by. Good-by.*

His father moves on legs leagued to catch the sun (that has pretended staying put while sneaking an imp ahead), and he brims wastefully in his father's wake, past the conical sugarcane-thatched *fales* where nets still depend like dew, past the native store—bushknives, goggles, guitarstrings, tinned-California-sardines, bolts of hibiscus-print, and doors boltless to unthievery—past the white Christian mission where the French priest is up and washing for mass. *Good-by.* They leave one old man girded in tapa and a tattoo mesh, sitting in morning beneath a breadfruit tree. Crossing the stream that threads umbilically a leaf on a vine on a hillside to oceans, they leave above the bridge two earlyboys to stoning their breakfast crabs (one hales up a limp fat backless one) and below the bridge a woman to pounding her laundry, wringing it, sending froth downstream.

The journey's beginning ends with the end of the village. Here is the last native fale. Somewhere near, a mountain will bound up trying to shake off its complex of creepers and runners andcrawlers canesstalksstemsandvines and mossesblossoms, ferns, tendrils and intrigues, though it can never leap that high, so many weigh it down, and its only foot is so balked in the tricks of the sea floor. Somewhere near, a trail will start to snarl its irritable way, getting snagged in lianas and wound around a sudden sapling.

Well, the horses are not quite here yet (though he hears them approaching—their shoeless hooves—and Tufele the guide swearing them on in soft Samoan) and so he can have a moment's rest. He has had to span nine yards and seven sights, smells and sounds to his father's one. His father moves in a more practical fashion.

His breathing subsides and then his heart mobs up. He laughs meaninglessly or perhaps with the eager pain of himself (so that his father wonders), but he must laugh and be. This is his journey. To where? To what he does not know? Men journey to nations and destinations and destinies and this is his journey.

He diverts a trickle of sweat from behind his knee with a switch, picks up a cool pebble to suck on, continuing a rhythm begun somewhere by the sea, and he is ready.

Tufele comes from the bush with his two charges. He grins. He has had to hunt them, lasso them; now he leads them on ropes of rough coir fiber. They do not want to follow. They have come down from the hill, their long flanks molten where the wet branches have hailed them. They had been pasturing along the stream, cropping at the edge of water, sometimes drinking in the darkest eddies, slowly monumentally pushing their noses up against the current. One is white, yellow-maned, one brown with blackened hocks. They are reluctant, beautiful in their contrary natures. They take insolent stances, three-hooved, as Tufele throws the pads onto their backs, cinches beneath their broad-veined bellies, slips his ropes in knotty halters behind their ears, around their sloped noses.

Eyes widening, neck arching imperiously, the white endures his father's mounting. And then his father draws him up onto that vault of rage, and his breath stutters although he is perched secure between his father's legs. His father clicks his tongue. The horse moves like doom above the earth, its bones heaving in the slow fires of its flesh.

(The blades in its shoulders slide like oars.) They leave the fale and rise into the forest, so that while climbing the path he can see through a momentary fissure in the trees the village sinking below (its brown thatches barely balancing on his fingertip, and his father's house, wrinkled tin and all, crashing from his nail into the shallows). —A sweep of blue to douse his eyes in.— Then morning is gone. They move on, ascending with the moist heat.

The horse's huge ribs force his knees out regularly. On a steeper incline he feels its breath break over into his ankle-bones, surge up his calves, loop in an ache across his thighs, so that he frequently has to shift. The sweat in his shins loosens, stirs with the horse's; in the small of his back loom the wets and washes of his father's loins. And the sunlight too foams down, welling or withdrawing among the pebbled branches as he and his father and Tufele on their horses move beneath the trees.

He rides upward, beginning to fit more truthfully to his horse, to merge with it, to rise and relent in the swells of its breaths, to move among it! And now he is filled with a strange love and belonging to his horse and for all things that are his horse, and he strokes his horse so that it will know it.

Suddenly he is amazed to see a knob of bone, pale and bloodless as in last night's dream, pulsing up from the beast's vertebrae. It throbs upward. It pierces his hand. He cannot move. And held as he is, in such oneness with his horse, he is aware of motion, passage, of the gestures of sunlight how it filters to a green flux through translucencies of leaves, splashes aquamarine down the smooth boles of ironwood, surges across the hushed mosses, swirls, assaults the horn to erode it, and pools restlessly, iridescently along the horse's neck and in and out of
  its mane,
and of trees cascading the lengths and shafts of their trunks
and of stones strangely floating and branches breaking adrift
  (in his mouth the pebble is churning, scuttling along his
  teeth)
and of the horse's mane swaying, green strands, soft seaweeds,
  and arching and then drifting down the horse's swarming
  flanks

and of the horse noiselessly running
liquid and lunging and waterswift
and of its legs running. Silent. Running.

Its ears are back; in its neck the rods lengthen. Sprigs of saliva burst at its lip. He watches one hot delicate fleck scurry to his knee. Why does it stop there; why does it simply float at his knee? In the horse's chest the mountains surge and crumple in mute tumult. Joints wrench like storms through the white nights of their sockets. Its forelegs, wrist-thin, are flurries of impulse. The horse's great sides heave, hover and heave, but now he hears no breathing. The horse's hooves, plunging, swirling, shatter no stones in its path. Then he sees it there; it is easy to see it: the beetle. Diminutive, heedless beside those thronging hooves, the beetle balances its olive hull in the angled frames of its legs, motionless, on a moldy green leaf. It is wearing a spittle collar.

And the horse hurtles, mounted in its gallop like a voice hung on one syllable. And the thick upper legs pump and splurge and swell in the pomp of their muscle, and the beetle does not move. High upon its crisp legs it is motionless. He would have shouted. He would have asked that beetle.

He opens his mouth; the hooves fall to the earth; the beetle sweeps away. The bone that had held him corrodes and shatters; a tear moves in his eye. He clutches at a branch as though at a name, but its leaves swish through his grasp. They are sharp-edged. One leaf severs the heel of his palm. In the moment that he sees it, before it touches air, his blood is green.

He blinks. Somewhere suddenly above, a bird flees that might have made announcement. His father tells him to be careful, if he should fall asleep he may fall from the horse. His father says, *You didn't sleep well. You turned in your sleep last night.* And the horse, though now it is only walking, breathes. But why does the horse curve its neck to the side that way (is it just that his father has reined it to make it turn?) and out of the edge of its great eye look at him? He leans far out onto the neck, grasping the derelict strands, and listens. But the horse is intent upon climbing. Only some flies perform a motley chant upon its neck and then in his wound.

His father tells him to sit up and be careful and let him see that hand. There is a rivulet of red that issues from his palm. It glistens in the sunlight and branches delicately when he moves his hand. His father reins in the horse and looks at the hand and then opens his doctor kit, needles and tongue-sticks and sealed gauzes, and cracks a seal. His father cleans the wound, swabs it, wraps a white gauze over it. (Should he? Should he tell his father?) His father orders him to take care of that hand or it may become infected; might become a yaw, even.

(That the sunlight was green, and the horse was running through it, and he and the horse belong. Should he?)

Coming down the far side of the mountain, halfway down it, they stop for lunch. It is already past noon, and time to eat. Besides, the day is at its hottest now and it is good to rest. They stop beside a brook that is narrow and clear and rimmed with ferns and the hairs of roots and overlapped with ruins. They tie their horses (when the horses have cooled they will let them drink, though not all they want) and Tufele drinks from the narrow brook and he and his father drink from their canteen.

(That the horse really was running and the beetle had crisp

legs and was motionless, and he almost knows something. Should he?)

He and his father eat tinned meat and biscuits and also the cake his mother had baked them and an alligator pear and greenish oranges and small orange mangoes and drink from their canteen. And Tufele sits on his heels and switches with a leafy branch the mosquitoes off his back and eats crisp baked green bananas and taro and a part of a breadfruit (it is good, that breadfruit; it is better than bread) and poi made of copra and reefwater wrapped in banana leaves. They give Tufele a slice of tinned meat and some cake and Tufele gives him a crisp banana and a piece of breadfruit and he eats them and drinks from the canteen, and Tufele drinks from the brook, holding the ferns aside to get to it. But when they get down the mountain a way, they will be able to drink the prickly-sweet water of young coconuts. Tufele will strap a belt about his ankles and scramble up a palm and then twist the coconuts off and let them drop and then scramble down, lop off their tops with his bushknife, and they will all drink as much as they want.

(What, what, *what* does he almost know?)

(Men journey.)

While his father and Tufele try to rest if they can among the rivalry of flies and reveling mosquitoes, *he* lies on a decaying green log across the brook (bark and punk fall into the brook, and some small white lizard eggs and a hazel centipede) and with a miniature noosed rod shaped of a spine of palm-leaf he dips into the brook, among the root-hairs, and patiently carefully snares a shrimp. Pale, lucid, the shape of water but for the thin line in the ridge of its tail, a jellied diamond, the shrimp sparkles and snaps its tail in the light. He has played this game before, with Sa'ii. He throws it back and tries for another. (If he told his father, his father would not believe.)

They untie their horses and let them drink and then mount them. It is steep going, down. His horse does not look back. They ride down-trail, facing the breeze that is moving up the mountain from the sea.

The trail follows the brook. Though sometimes they leave the brook to go around a fallen tree or over a rise of verdant lava, they always return to it. And the brook moves to the sea. On the hillsides about them, water seeps from the ground, rustling the fern stems, carrying particles of lava and decayed plant, and flows down the hillsides to sluice across their trail and swell the brook that moves to the sea. Now the forest begins to hold back. They pass through a grove of palms and then through more open expanses so that they are for whole moments fully in sunlight. And now he can smell the sea, the slow medicinals of its brine, tinctures of cast shell and seaweed; now he hears it—they ride out of a cane brake onto a coral beach into the full bloom of sunlight. The beach is narrow because the tide is full, and the brook fans out over it, pushing debris —twigs and splinters, the pink white purple black halves of infinitesimal clamshells, bric-a-brac, broken bleached hieroglyphs of the reef, and perhaps also a limp damp spider—and slips gratefully into the Pacific. The seabreeze chuckles through the tops of the rimming palms. The sea tosses what is left of its greenfoam breakers onto the beach.

There are nine Samoans waiting at the edge of the sea. They are here already, standing in the foam to manage their longboat, their lavalavas drenched so that their nakedness shines through, beads of spume glistening and drying on their arms.

They stand on each side of the longboat or at its stern and the breakers push the stern above the beach and they let it lift and then let it slide back on the receding water. Tufele calls *Talofa!* to them, and they wave (always with one hand on the boat) and laugh and call *Talofa!*

They have come to take him and his father. They have been waiting, with the sea.

The chief among them strides from the breakers, trailing the surf like a snail-path from his body. The chief is tall, lank-muscled, with long grooves curling from the edges of his eyes, and a loop of fat snuggling his waist. He is tattooed blue from the small of his back to his knees. The chief speaks in half-English to his father and then in Samoan to Tufele. Tufele grins and speaks to the chief, and then suddenly the chief looks down upon *him,* quietly, strangely with something gentle in his eyes. And the chief laughs, gently. The chief is wearing a green leaf in his hair.

The chief lifts him, and speaks Samoan, and carries him to the longboat and laughs and speaks Samoan and sets him in the boat. Along the gunnels the natives laugh. The boat rollicks and rocks in the sea's romping tickle, and as he founders its length, over the thwarts and helter-skelter oars, he is warmed in the praises of laughter (these people who stand in the sea and praise with their laughter), and the sea strokes its long hand beneath the keel, coaxing the longboat. The spray flicks its light prelude onto his neck.

The chief speaks. Two men leap from the side of the boat and run to his father. They shape a chair with their arms and lift the doctor up and carry him to the boat. Then again the chief speaks, sharply. The crew scramble into the boat, their

lavalavas drizzling, their naked feet sloshing onto the thwarts: scuffle, clatter of lifted oars banging blades, thump of oak to metal as oars are popped into locks, creak of oarlocks dickering in their swivels, horse's whinny, crackle of breakers collapsing and then their soughing back, shift of bilge, spray's-spatter, foam's swarm, fizz,
and then the winglike poise of the eight oars dripping sea,
and the sixteen arms unflexed, ready, the eight backs hunched with expectancy: slow lift of the bow, the chief's shout and shove,
and grind of stern upon coral as the chief leaps aboard,
and the boom and bend of the oars,
the rigid jerk of the longboat,
the surge seaward as they are free.

His father sits in the stern-sheets. The chief stands beside his father, full of benign flourish, tall, demonstrative in the pride of his place, chanting the stroke to the rowers, steering the longboat grandly by the sweep lashed to the stern. The spines of the rowers crook in their backs as they rock forward and laugh and then pull, laugh; the blades fall with one sound into the sea, sweep sternwards, lift, tossing berries of spray in the air.

But on the beach astern sits Tufele. The horses stand, heads down, manes drooping. Tufele waves, and he waves to Tufele, who grows smaller and smaller waving from the beach and gradually disappears between the breakers and the trees. And the hectic collapse and coughing noise of the breakers too diminishes. The roll of the surface beneath them is longer, more assured, as they glide above the reef.

He leans out over the bow, to see. The bow falls away from his eyes, curving neatly into the sea; and the sea, cut by the stem, rises in a thin cool sheath up the sides of the bow and curls outward and falls. He reaches down with his bandaged hand as far as he can, disrupting the top arch of its pattern. His father tells him, *Keep that bandage dry*. But below him sweep the sunken still forests of the reef, lime thickets, brittle arbors, mushrooming plateaus, beds of blossoms that are the mouths of worms, sea cucumbers, tanglings of slick weed. Below him a silver-striped maonofish pastures on the crusty branches; a mincing yellow-and-green spiny lobster backs half seen beneath a ledge.

A community of small intense fish is patrolling the reef in soundless urgency. The bow dips. They dart an unscattered precise angle and away.

Suddenly the longboat has shot beyond reef's-end and is taking the full ocean, mounting the blue backs of mammoths. It startles him, this abrupt dismissal of all land, plunge to nowhere, new dominion of unending depth, for he can see the reefwall how it plummets headlong down pitching straight to darkness like the fall of a full music into silence. The sunlight fluctuates among the upper shelves, muted, and then beneath dapples wanely an undercropping here and there, and the subdued longer rays sound softly through twilight into the dome of that deep night downward.

They teeter atop a crest, totter; the keel slips; the longboat noses down into the trough, yahooing at the bow. He squeezes the gunnel timbers in his grip. The night opens beneath him. But he will never let go. He will squeeze the splinters of this gunnel right down onto the floor of that night, if he must. But the subtle dome retreats. The bow wallops into the foot of the next swell, flinging the joke and spray in his teeth, surging him up to the next summoning summit, atop it—the sun and the upper sea! Swung in the white bright hull and hold of this boat, the fro and to of the rowers their cradling backs—the sun and the upper sea!

His father is laughing. He looks toward the stern. That is when the stern lifts, towering the chief against the sky. In the chief's tall head the eyes shine like suns, and they are looking at him.

The stroke-oar unfeathers and showers the chief with a crab of spray. As though it were an act of supreme dignity, the chief lets the water stream down until his body glistens alive with it. High above the tumbling brown backs of the rowers looms the chief, in a skin of flame—sea amber, sun wash. The chief speaks once, in Samoan. With a great wrenching stroke the rowers launch the bow above the sea.

The oars halt, straight out like beetle legs. All the hardware is hushed, rib, timber, brace and bolt still. Then, like something out of last night's dream, the rowers turn to *him,* and raise their soft brown faces. On all their faces the sea is trickling, sweat-like, so that their faces are alive with it, cheek and nose and brow, and they are not laughing. They are looking at him.

The eyes that see are shining on his hand. He looks down at his hand. The wet gauze falls off (medicine and dead blood upon it like an unreal negative), and his hand glows in the light. The revealed wound is like an island in his hand, green, he is sure it is green, and glistening at its edges with the wet. And
he can sense

the greenwings scooting high on the winds of his breath,
finny and greengilled wheelings in his veins,
and his hands' clammy hinges opening green, green—
shell and coral spell of his bone.

He would have shouted. He would have asked those rowers.

His mouth opens; the hull shakes; the bow falls shuddering into the sea. He gasps. Spray bounces upon the thwarts, drenches his body, shatters in the bilge. The west sun is back. His father, whose face is wet with spray and who is wiping it now with a handkerchief, looks up, startled. And the rowers pull at their oars, laugh, break into song,

I'm going to my loving home
with my eyes full of tears
sweet love so dear to me
Oi a peli fa sili sili,

and to starboard the island dances upon the waves.

His father calls him to come to the stern and let him see that hand. He rises, balancing in the bow, all drenched and questioning, and his father laughs at the sight of him. He crawls to the stern between the rowers bowing and pulling at their oars, and holds out his naked hand to his father. (Should he? Should he tell?) His father tells him to take off his tennis shoes and shorts, and helps him with his shoes. He balances on the stern-sheet and takes off his soaked shorts, and then he is naked; the crew is singing. The shoes and shorts are put to dry across the first thwart. Because it is growing evening, his father wraps his own shirt about him and takes him upon his lap and puts an arm around him, and together these two rise and fall in the stern of the longboat. Until suddenly he is telling his father everything. How the white horse ran on the mountain, and its green mane, and how a moment ago this boat hung so still above the water, for his sake. And his green palm. Why? Why was it green? And why? And why?

His father laughs and tousles his hair, and winks at the rowers.

His father says, *Let me see that hand.* Then his father cleans it, swabs it red, puts a new gauze over it. His father tells him, *Now listen. You don't know what in the water comes off these beaches. And when you're playing, climbing trees with Sa'ii, you don't know what comes off the bark of those trees. Or eating Tufele's breadfruit, even, the way you did at lunch. Can't you remember that?* his father says. *Can't you learn that at all?*

The rowers are rowing silently.

Father, he asks, *was the horse really running?* His father laughs, *Of course!* laughs, tousles his hair.

But it is evening now, and his thoughts are like that. He is strangely subdued. And maybe because he has been all afternoon upon the sea, the sea is merely the sea, something outside this hull, and quieter, now that they are on the lee of the island.

The bow turns toward land, where the trees are darkening. The crew row silently through a narrow channel and without adventure across a still reef. Two or three lights from a village blink through the twilight. He can make out the dark hulks of native fales; he can just barely hear the tide withdrawing from a beach. As they move nearer, he hears another sound—a soft murmuring that mixes with the tide sounds and then gradually becomes distinct. It is voices.

With a muffled rasp the bow grounds onto the beach. A crowd of natives are on the beach—girls and small boys like Sa'ii (many of them with babies nodding on their hips), and men, and women. They talk softly. The older boys and the men come down to pull the longboat up onto the beach. The crew step over onto the damp beach and help him and his father out of the boat. While he and his father wait upon the beach, the longboat is beached. The oars are given to boys to carry; the longboat is carried keel-up and placed high upon the beach, beneath a palm. The last sea water dribbles down the clinkers of the upturned hull, and pits the sand beneath. Up in the palm there is a night wind blowing.

It is dusk now. He can barely see the chief. The chief speaks in half-English to his father. His father nods and slings on the medicine kit and tells him to follow. The chief speaks Samoan; the semicircle of natives parts, and he and his father follow the chief up from the beach and through the village. Many of the natives on the beach follow after. In the village, in some of the fales, there are kerosene lanterns. And where there are those lights, he can see the natives watching from between the shiny wooden pillars.

One or two small urchins run ahead. Their cousins dart after them, catch them, whisper to them.

At last they come to a dark bulky place—pricked in the lower half with stars, it seems to him. Here he and his father and the chief stop. His eyes adjust, and he sees that it is a huge native fale. Unlike those other dwellings they had passed, this one has its mats all down between the pillars. Then he sees that the stars are rays of light needling their way outward between the rough weave of the mats. And now he hears, issuing from deep within the fale, a strange dull distant hum.

The chief speaks a command in Samoan. The natives turn and walk back through the darkness to their fales.

The chief looks down at him and then at his father. His father hesitates a moment. Then his father nods.

The chief lifts up a mat. They go in.

Inside, a lantern hangs upon a post. It lights the whole fale. Above them, the concave dome of the fale is like a dark cup, covering them, holding them in. A mosquito net hangs in the center of the fale. Its edges are tucked beneath a mat. Suspended from its one thong, the net is a fragile pyramid. And the net quivers with myriad black specks that rise and swarm and re-land with a dry buzz. They are flies. His ears are filled with that humming.

His father goes to the net. It is fear that makes him follow his father. He doesn't want to go to that net. His father touches the net. Suddenly the flies are up from it, buzzing, buzzing, buzzing grossly about them. His father lifts the edge of the net.

And who is she, who sits there, silent, looking at him? Why is she looking at *him?* Darkness is in her eyes. She sits straight and condemned and graceful upon the mat, her legs smooth and crossed, her dark hands lying patiently upon her knees, and she is looking at him. Her black hair cascades her shoulders and her breasts. It is darker than the deepest sea.

And what on her face
is the green terrible kiss
whose pebbled sticky bloom oozes and glistens
in the lantern light? It has eaten her nose
all open to the bone. And where
her lips had been, her teeth shine through.

And this, his father says from somewhere in the dark, *this on her face is what the island is.*

And she beautifully slowly closes her eyes, and she opens them slowly, beautifully. Her eyes are quiet, dark and deep. When he looks that deeply into them, he knows that she is more than at peace; she is at one. She is unquestioning.

Then, angrily, with his father moving somewhere in the dark, he looks down upon his own hand, and rips up the gauze, and rages to see: already it has begun to heal.

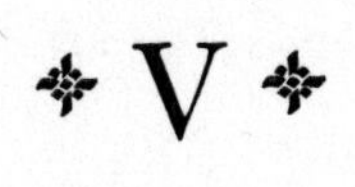

The Ants

How long wilt thou sleep, O sluggard?
When wilt thou arise out of thy sleep?

I

Thus was our City built. And I have traveled, even through the vetch and farthest edges of the grass, and there is no other like it. Perfect it was, in its every structure: the singular and just accomplishment of our labor. Forum and basilica! the Halls of Incubation and cool crypts of storage, treasuries and stockyards, nurseries, granaries, concourses, hothouses and cellars. And central to it all, that *Queenschamber*, high vaulted dark place, beamed of an ancient bone. Imagine the fervor, the press of body and consultative stroking of feeler that went into the working of this room. With what a cunning and ant skill, with what subtlety of architecture was that rib caused to abut a lump of stone and sustain delicately the whole soil's thrust. Nowhere have I seen its counterpart. This was a chamber sacred in the earth; here were stately motions, majestic posturings, the sceptral gestures of a Queen's regal abdomen amid the devout attendance and ecstasy of Her retinue. The minting of our City's wealth.

How shall I tell the beauty of my City, all passageways, all chambers harmoniously arranged, and all obstructions transmuted to purposeful architecture, even to the deepest suburb? Some ceilings were compact of soil; some were the cool undersides of fieldstone. Here and there a root or pebble buttressed a wall. In one room a piece of sharp glass divided the floor, and its edge gave pleasure to whoever passed over it.

This was our City.

And think on the wisdom of that fabled Queen, our City's Founder, how once upon an antique swarming-time She flew Her nuptials highest in the sun, taking the worthiest mate, and from Her tall brief vista elected this site. Here was a dampish soil choicest for building, and a precinct bountiful in grassgrain and succulent brood of insects and the ground-clinging purslane whose bruised stems yield water. Foremost of all, here grew that sumac so vital to our prosperity. The remainder of the meadow is level; there is no other bush; the Queen, myth of our beginnings, came down to demonstrate love by rubbing off her wings and settling to the east of this bush, and it was our greatness. For the sun rose in the east to touch our City; citizens stirred under the first fingers of heat and warmed to happy labor, bustling in the nurseries or stringing from the nest down its long steaming sides to forage in the still gloomy dandelion groves. And although by noon the expansive sun had pressed down to blunt the ant tribes roundabout so that their work was short and came to nothing, our sumac protected us. We persisted, laboring in its shade up to the cool dusk.

See my sisters toiling in that golden age: sunlight, and the straw-glistening City: the diverse business, hustlebustle, traffic, congestion, gesticulation, the commerce and mirth of it! A team of six amber-bodied ants lugs a beetle backwards, thirty-six blond feet gripping and slipping against the freight while the iridescent bald hull progresses or slides back upon the mound. Here prances a proud ant, advances with a cargo of dying mayfly, whose wings flicker and trip her into a dusty somersault. And another, mincing in short six-steps to the summit, a scrap of blackberry in her jaws. Now the milkmaids come from the pastures where they have been herding their aphids browsing on the vines. They have groomed and pampered the stock, and tapped the great green bellies to wheedle a drop. Now these clever aphidpunchers' crops are full of a healthful sweet honeydew, to feed our City.

From five directions, highways approach the City. On each a gang of keenjawed amber worksisters is snipping stubble to keep the thoroughfare cleared. Here comes a procession of graingatherers up a highway now, back from their field day. The ground stirs with the flickings of their feet: a fine harvest! Now they sweep joyously by, lordly in labor, each heavy with the sweet odor of work, each displaying a splendid grassseed. What titillation of tall antennae, up like pennants! How bright the gold guerdon of the new grain! Where have you traveled, among what ants have you witnessed a greatness to compare to this, in enterprise or accomplishment? It was work did this, and the exigencies of earth. The ant is no witless thing such as winged brutes are, those beings that fly, that move through distance and distance without obstacle, a wandering in air and a continual forgetfulness. But we, who are of the earth, are not like this. The earth knows us, and we keep the memory of it. There is a closeness in everything. For us there is no journey that does not have its starting place. And of all ants, we built the noblest.

But glory is brief. It must be always new won. Complacency spoils it like a fungus. Those days my City! days of harvesting and chaste good work, a terse laboring in sunlight, all my golden sisters willing and worthy, soon enough would be ended.

Though none then knew it.

11

Hour upon hour our Queen spun out a rich spawn. It was the measure of Her regality. Her eggs hatched; her larvae co-cooned into numerous strong daughters, who labored. But in the meadow, though so many more ants gathered, they gathered less. And it was seen with what increasing boldness barbarians trespassed our domains, zones particular to us, where grain grew. And ladybugs and gall wasps were more numerous than had ever been remembered. Thieving was in our fields and rapine among our herds. Often an aphid was found gaping, half-eaten. And there were other aphids, milked by stealth, who could yield nothing to us.

We bred soldiers, for we saw we must. Certain larvae were reared in a warm room: heat quickens growth and makes a large ant. To stiffen their jaws, these grubs were fed only rough fragments of seed—and somewhat less than they hungered for, so as not to evolve a full female, but rather one just short of it: a fierce thing: a soldier. Their mandibles could puncture, and bludgeon, and cleave even a twig.

We put our dreadnaughts to duty, for more than ever there were subtle rustlings, marauders questing through the grass. And one day, after we had roved all morning from pilfered to pilfered stalk and come at last on good pickings, we caught a whole crew at it. I was witness to this. The instant they smelled us they began skidding down the stalks. So many fell that it was like waterdrops, the way wind shakes them from leaves after rain. Those who relinquished their stolen grain in time, got free; the rest were slain where they sprawled, their gray abdomens and thoraxes twitching in separation, punctuating the thin sunlight that filtered barlike through the thicket.

We workers would have been content with collecting the abandoned grain. But our soldiers never halted, but charged after the escaping pillagers so that we had to follow. We came to the enemy's city, nest of thieves, which was strong with their smell, harsh and spicy, and we workers feared to do more. Also, we were anxious to gather the largess scattered behind us. But suddenly a soldier lunged into the open, and reared and pranced. Her jaws snapped and snatched as if singly to affright the enemy. Then she ran back to her soldiersisters and passed from one to another, peppering them with her feelers. Twice she did this, and we workers could not understand it. But all about us the soldiers began to make taut nervous cries with their legs and to slam their gasters at the ground, raising spurts of dust to hover in a haze above us. Then abruptly, in a body, they rushed across the clearing and down the sandy funnel and into the nest. O the sun shone in silence; no breeze confused the grass. But the ground jerked with a dark violence that stabbed up through our tibias and became a terror within us.

Now a gray ant's head popped up, and some of us fled. And another and another and another gray head. The funnel seethed with those ants. Most hauled cocoons or pupae, dragging them through the dust. One of them rushed amongst us, paused, then began circling in bewilderment. We saw that she had lost her feelers. Six of us seized her, by leg, by neck, by abdomen; she became a maddened thing; I carry scars for this. But she did not go free. And others, when they smelled who we were, turned and ran.

Our soldiers, feverish with triumph, marched forth into the sunlight. They were laden with grain, a treasure of it. And when we returned to our City, the halls shook with excitement. Our sisters felt how richly laden we were and how ripe and plump and dry the new grain and so much of it, and the City was thrown into turmoil and rejoicing. *Celebration! Celebration!* All the little rituals of delight! Tweedlings, jigglings our tibias together, glad small trills from our legs' clefs wrung, dittyrambs, laud songs of joy and stridulation. Frolics and frisks all kithy and kinny, knotsandclumps, risings up to a rapturous sisterhood, tupsy-turvy, all trysted together, fumbling, sistering, darling one another. Tingling antennae, what a spree! Bumpt, butted, bunched, blent, thumpt floors with our gasters, whisked our musty passes through the dust; bobs of, clusters of, in teems, in pairs, tipsy-daisying up to oneanother to feed and knead oneanother, one clungtoone, tight, it was a lovely plight! Pats and flatterings to woo regurgitation. Sweetmeats of grain or syrupy pabulum. Pushing it all through oneanothers' palps. Until our crops were filled and tender—and we were contented newlyfeds!

III

So the barbarians were punished. And others also. Big lemon-hued avengers, invincible antada, our army crushed into nest after nest. Grain was found hoarded in most of those nests.

But the army grew. The City was soon overrun with soldiers. We felt them in every chamber, obstacles, heavy-headed, large-sullen-bodied, who did nothing but bide the next battle and be fed and cause death to many workers from the sheer fatigue of tending them, or from the dumb peevish maulings that we sometimes received. And where once we had gone forth to harvest in liberty, to thread our curiosity through the grass and mount the bent shafts and pluck the good seed, or come on a mammothy grasshopper of greens and browns brought down—who knows how—for our nutriment, or to drag an amber gum off thistles, so that it was all to our glory, we learned soon enough how soldiers reserve all glory to themselves. And one afternoon during a raid, after the soldiers had scoured an enemy nest and found not a grassgrain there, they seized those cocoons that had been left abandoned, softer than grassseed, in the deserted runways.

Ant eggs, those of an enemy, are delicacies to eat. The soldiers were quick to discover this. After a first taste they would eat nothing else, nor permit us to either, they were so domineering. And because an ant egg is smaller than their gross jaws can handle, we workers had duteously to pan each damnable dainty into the soldiers' mouths. We would rather have been free. And once upon a warm night, while harm seemed hunting otherwhere, breathless in the parched grass, and while my City lay still, isolate, and of a smell of sleeping, and soldiers' slept heads were drowsome, ponderous, pillowed across oneanothers' torsos, and in corridors, in the dark corridors, in what places we could, we workers slept or semislept upon steads of our legs, pressing ourselves to restfulness against the walls, and night lay her summersdark hand longfingered onto earth, earth's heat expiring upward like one breath against it, and if there were any stirrings anywhere we did not know of it—only remote signals of reclusive crickets, black lyricists of night whose intermittencies fumbled our sleep—down in the granary where those captured eggs were stacked waiting to be eaten, *something stirred, hatching, pod-bursting, to squeak through a split jacket from its own silence and into that night.*

In the morning we found an ant there, vigorous of antennae, atop those eggs.

IV

White callow, how could we have felt you from our own? You were soft and milky and smelled fragrant like one of ours. In time you passed through an amber phase, flaxen-feelered, your legs edged with rust: much like us. But when at last you went up into the sunlight, you turned out gray—we should have killed you then! But it was too late; you had already ingratiated yourself with the soldiers, truckling to them, mealymouthing them, fawning their arrogance all over as if they deserved it. Rear guard, tidying after their soldierly discharges.

I suspect you. You worked long hours, but mostly down among those eggs: bringing forth rations to your mistresses. That wasn't all you brought forth. Hatchings increased; soon every third ant was gray, though smelling just like us. And these devoted themselves entirely to the soldiers, who now between their wars cared for nothing but luxury. This the gray ants zealously furnished them. But we who had lived classics of labor and known the sweetness and the glory of this, because we despised deferring to some soldier's whim, were peremptorily demoted, our heads snappished off.

Some of us left—I cannot tell that ant ache—forsaking the high mound, the intricate chambers, and all else we had been. To work, in the wilderness, in our own way. But what is toil (though its motions sing) that has for its purpose nothing greater than one's single survival, which ends, soon? We were few. We had no queen. And from such a distance we watched what I spell out now, in this history.

V

Day upon day, by morning, by noon, by evening, the elect—those generalissimas, my proud soldiersisters—mustered in the noblest chamber and prepared. All about them in the nest the dusky slaves, the gray ones, stored food or cleaned halls or tended the eggs and cocoons. But these hulkheaded tsarinas in-exerted themselves; in keen tactical strategical upperechelonals of comfort passed the long hours; burnished their upperbrassy limbs, rust-edged members beautiful in length, puissant, stippled with short blond hairs. Long hours they spent combing their feelers with their forelegs, between the spur and bristled tarsal, and then currying the legs themselves through their mouthparts, over and over, all the long hours, and with such élan that there was not a blemish left. Then they would go spotlessly to sleep—by platoon, by regiment, by squadron: easy aces: great ants (for sleep): dauntless (in dozing).

The soldiers relieved this militant regimen only with fighting, which by now they had brought to perfection. All else was decay. And after a space of quiet, when all that peacefulness would become oppressive and begin to irk them so that they fretted among themselves, dreaming up an anger, and the mere beheading or behinding of a slave here and there was not enough to content them, the soldiers would heave their great heads half awake and lift their magnificent amber bodies and march up through the passageways like rumblers of doom. Or sometimes, if the burden of their sleep seemed as though it might weigh them down forever, the gray ants themselves went in amongst them, stirred them up a little, pinched and provoked them, pulled at their legs until finally the agonized dreadnaughts would lash about in fierce amber rage and snap at the walls and ceilings, and then nothing could stop them; in a moment they would reassemble outside the nest, seemingly half in a daze, then suddenly fuse, thorax to thorax, and *run!* through the grass.

Most often the army stormed the mother nest of the gray ants. It was easiest. Repeated conquest had made those ants abject. The gray ants would simply cower in their nest, not resisting at all, and let the raiders take whatever they wished. And back at the City, if the army had sacked the nest of the grays, and returned reeking of that place, then they were greeted excitedly and petted and fed; and the gray slaves took those eggs. But if it was another nest that the soldiers had raided, then (it was no matter what suffering they had paid to victory nor how many sisters they had left doubled in death behind them) no gray ant would touch the soldiers; not a slave would feeler them; they were left to go to their room with the ache of unstrokeness on their bodies. And down in Her chamber, beneath the bone, surrounded by those alien and attentive slaves, how could my old sparse Queen, still hopefully spawning, have guessed what was happening? A few of Her eggs, it is true, were allowed to hatch. But these were always soldiers, giant white callows who were led to lay their milky abdomens down amongst their sisters and discover sloth. However, if a gray ant was hatched (from those eggs the army had fetched), then the moment it had hardened it would be brought to labor. It would be taught the raking of an earthcrumb with its jaws, and how to assist a grub in cocooning, and in the cool granaries how to check the grain against mildew. Out in the meadow, under all that light, it would be taught to drag at a blackberry, and to bite a pea off vetches. And these gray ants, when they were at last mature, roved the meadow, threads of safari through the jungleish chickweed, between mushroom mesas, beneath the sahara of a saltbush. They were searching.

VI

One day she came to them.

It was a day in late spring, that time of root-ramming, when pea vines put out a tendril stranglehold on spring, when something growing turns a stone in its socket. By then, many-pronged rain has forced the sexual flowers. Flying things fill the air. And one—winged, dark as death or victory—appeared at the nest. At the entrance her wings fell off, four thin, veined transparencies structured like a fable, which the wind blew away. Then this gray female entered, meek as any slave.

The gray ones pretended she was not there, she was so quiet. The soldiers when they met her took her for a joke, teased her in hopes that she might defend herself and give them an incentive to bite her head off. But she never resisted. She lay for hours enduring their cruelties. Then when her submissiveness had bored them stiff, the soldiers would go back to sleep. So for a week this ghostly one wandered slowly about the City, always patient, never offensive, exploring room after room and the dark hallways. At last she came to the Queenschamber. Ah! Pretend this assignation was a thing of state, that an antique Empress, weary, weary, weary of Her realm, wrecked, toothless, all the wonder gone out of Her, Her crowning fecundity—that had held Her queen and prisoner—now almost totally diminished from grace, received this other as deliveress. And that this other recognized a peer, was gracious (pretend that queens in any species can be royal), was munificent as queens should be. It does not matter. In a day the Old Queen was dead. That gone Paragon, that scratched Sovereign stately and stiff, the whole inch of Her yet a queen, was drummed up through the passageways. Her golden scars glinted in the sunlight from which She had so long been kept. They laid Her in the grass and left Her there, to bleach into monument. In time even this collapsed, without ceremony.

VII

The stolid steadfast soldiers preened.

And they preened and they preened and they preened. But now the slaves paid them no attention whatsoever. Those gray ants were elsewhere. They were out gathering grain, or shepherding their aphids. Down in the Queenschamber, they were attending ecstatically the stately motions, majestic posturings, gray sceptral gestures of a queen's regal abdomen.

The mighty mistresses grew hungry, but no ant came to serve them. A flunky passing through would either have no food or, if it had, it would not yield it. Of course it would be killed, to teach it a lesson. But in that case, whatever food it had would stay like a knot in its crop; the soldiers would be left licking their stubby tongues on air. Then what a fury they would be in! They would tear the ceiling to shambles. No slave would come to clean it. The soldiers would run through the halls, ripping the dark, furiously butting pebbles, and some would be in such a rage that they would spend days bitten to a rootstalk, to teach it a lesson. Yet, though desperate, they remained proud. It is always that way. The mighty admit no fault. But when *we* were builders, suffering to shape our City, we workers were full of flaws, and so we could labor for perfection. But the soldiers? Had not their foresisters raised this City for *them*, for their enjoyment? And were they not now a mighty ant, BIG, much to be respected, superior even in color, and in war always victorious?

They decided to stage a great raid (it had become all they knew to do) to make their world safe for luxury. But this time they would assault a different nest, seize a better slave, one that could evict these disobedient damned gray ants from the mound. That done, the new slaves would submit themselves to that highest authority, the soldier ants, and feed them, and even *raise* the standard of luxury.

The soldiers began to clean for action. They spent days getting themselves flashy for the fight. Each licked her legs and feelers a dozen sensual ways to raise them to martial luster—all spit-and-polish—and otherwise tidied her body. Proper grooming is vital in battle. And they sparred among themselves, practicing their tacticals, maneuvers and combaticals, attack! counterattack, with their mandibles rapiering eachother's rearguards until it tickled, assaulting oneanother's breastworks at close quarters, and other such war games. Occasionally they enlisted a chance slave for drill, and demonstrated correct procedure in performing a military operation on its flank, reducing its legs and antennae to so many fieldpieces. They sent out scouts into the meadow, and soon a scout might be glimpsed behind every pebble or grassstem, under every leaf: sly infiltrators taking security measurements. If any believed she had been detected, she would pretend craftily to be a worker, picking up a twig and dropping it.

VIII

Two or three spies came back with reports of a heathenish settlement on the butte of a rotting stump at the edge of the meadow. This was a nest reported to smell thickly of cocoons and eggs and yet to be garrisoned by only a small primitive corps of ants. The next afternoon, after a siesta, the soldiers mustered outside the City. *Tum tum tumtetum* they drummed their gasters at the ground, *feedoleedee feedoleedee* they stridulated their legs in fifey tremolos, parading up and down in review, feelers aloft, bodies dazzling lemonbright shouting back the light, sharp jaws glinting. O here was all a fierce beauty, had there been any onlookers to applaud it. But the gray ones were out in the fields, or down in the nest—going about their business as though that were the only glory, and war less than a breeze through the grass, now and again troubling it.

After a bit more flourish, the soldiers dispatched a division in the direction of the stump citadel; the rest marched into bivouac in the shade of their sumac, to rest.

IX

Guided by a scout who wound her way back on the spool of her memory—threads of odor and earth texture and tilt—the division advanced in quickstep to the target. At last they came to the barbarian stronghold, which stood in the midst of a bracken forest.

The soldiers surveyed the scene. The stump was barkless, weatherworn, presenting a perpendicular smooth bluff. But about its base grew woodsorrel, now in purple bloom, and broadleaved pigweed beneath which sappers could hide. A tough-vined Virginia creeper had crept almost to the summit, so that an ant could get a feethold. And farther up, there were fungus shelves and old woodpecker holes where the army might regroup and sustain its attack.

Reconnaissance had just been sent up a dandelion stem to confirm all this when a platoon of ants appeared upon the bluff. They were a red ant, ugly hairy things, and somewhat awkward for they were shortlegged. The soldiers instantly assumed invincible attitudes, high prancings, feintings toward the stump, rearings up in a most ant-awful fashion, spreadings wide of their jaws. The noise of their mandibles closing was like the pop of multitudinous blatant weedpods. Then the soldiers settled down to let the red ones flee. The red ones fled.

Right down the stump and at the soldiers! The generalissimas were forced to snip the clumsy creatures in half. But each red ant that died left a bitter mucus in its executioner's jaws. It was so fiery, an ant could hardly endure it. Then the crazed soldiers ran about with that fire in their jaws. And they were seized by other red ants, who would not let go. While the soldiers flung and trounced them, these scarlet perverts angled their abdomens under and *stung*. It was unfair. Once a soldier had been stung, her limbs cramped, her antennae quivered to paralysis, a froth dammed her mouth. Then she was immobile; death came slow.

The soldiers were stopped halfway up the stump. They began to be steadily driven down. Soon they were fighting at the base of the stump, amongst the woodsorrel and roots, and the rheumy casques and still members of the dead. They were in despair.

Then it was they had the miracle.

Then it was a god held over them, against the time of their trouble, and they came to know it. Then they were saved.

Two great trunks of doom appeared suddenly above the two armies, and rose heavenward to a fork, and higher, higher, to where the tall upthrusting divinity caught casts of late uplifted light. It was all unnamable, although a godly odor drifted down among the ants: as from strange places, other kingdoms, farther fields beyond this interformicine war.

Abruptly from that lofty fork, rebuking and wrathful, a burning rain came down, alive and single-stemmed, parting the light: hurled watery pillar, blazing and golden and twisting in the light, from that godhead. And the Word was made water. Refulgent, spattering, the fury blasted the reds, and scattered them. Coupled strugglers were divided by that acrid remonstrance. Confusion was everywhere. Rivers broke from fresh-created craters (the vengeance struck with such force), and channels were cleft—sluicing, gushing, flooding—astringent and yellow. The steams of censure rose.

The red ants fled. They had known the wrath, and they were dismayed.

Regathering at a distance, among fern trunks at the perimeter of the battlefield, the soldiers watched with awe as their Savior tucked away His almighty and walked, two-legged. Where the Earth-shaker trod, where His foot was set down, there was a whirlwind in the grass. And He went from them. And the soldiers were filled with rejoicing, for they had been saved.

They sent for reinforcements.

X

The meadow's shadows were expanding eastward against evening when the reinforcements arrived, the whole army through the twilight bracken. The remnants of the first division by now were prostrate from their extended hunger and from fear that those thorntailed devils might attack again. So they were joyous to greet their sisters and touch them all over with salutes. They let them taste their wounds, and smelled out to them the strange deaths of their poison-pricked comrades. And of the god's water, which was everywhere—blackening the stump, glistening in the fleece of dandelion caps. And how His rebuking rainfall had come golden. It was a portent. Right was on their side.

The army did not wait. They advanced to the stump. They hoped the red ants would flee, leaving their cocoons and eggs to the conquerors, for it seemed there might be a limit to the red ants' reserves. But the red ants rimmed the top of the stump and worked their feelers and waited. The stump's precipice was a perpendicular damp battlefield between the two armies. This space grew electric with expectancy. Small noises broke out here and there, nervous warriors inadvertently rasping their hackles. Then these cries were heightened to signals and challenges. Soon two dominant themes overbore, both of hate. Suddenly, as though a thorn were to split strenuous milkweed and free the cramped flosses, the upper ranks of the amber army burst: the soldiers swirled up the dead treefoot, crush and rush upward of myriad golden ants, sap welling honey-yellow from dry roots to force through into a leaf of victory.

But near the summit they were met by hairy demons. And in the bloody sunset they strove, back and forth. And some attained the summit and fought there. And some fought upon a fungus shelf, burning upon that cold mortality, or clung to the fungus undersides, pinched to oneanother, coupled in consummate loathing; and some head-downward slipped to catch to the defunct smooth muscles of the stump, in tight curls of hate wrestling, stinging, gnawing. And legs fell; heads, abdomens fell; often whole ants, stung stiff, fell; and often ants, in their extremity still paired, fell, their very faintness clinching them together. It was all done in silence; it was all done in the febrile orange stresses of the dwindler sun. Only, here and there, motions tenuous in the grass: cripples spinning on their wretched stubs.

About the base of the stump, the booty of war was heaped: red ants and golden: dead, dying: maimed, colorful. Hundreds were buckled to an immortal humbleness, bits and pieces of muscle gone into tremors, last echoes of a late swiftness. The bodies of hundreds of stung amber soldiers lay leg-upward in the rooty twilight, like casks of now static juices. It was pile upon pile of ant motion, layers of rich ant memory, sweet impulses, works of days, now all extinct. Thus the ants lay dead.

And the amber soldiers were driven down and had to retreat upon pontoons of comrade and enemy. Many were hindered by their dying sisters who, in their longing to be delivered somehow back to life, clutched them and hung to them. Others traversed dying reds, and were stung, and dragged their own fiery deaths a short way farther and then ceased and surrendered themselves to the tally.

XI

Through dusky fern, under cover of a rear guard, the soldiers retreated.

The rear guard was massacred.

Those ants who could, hobbled homeward to their City—a thin meager string of amber ants devoted entirely to desperation, straggling beneath the accomplished fern, under drooped and laden beards of grasses, and seeded chickweed, and the ripe drupes of blackberries. But when they arrived at their

City, their City towered above them in the night, and it it was not their City. Though the soldiers climbed to the usual height, they could hardly find the entrances. Those who did, found them to be of a strange conformation: funnel-shaped, small, very like the entrances to a nest of grays.

The soldiers were so feeble and dispirited, they could not push their heads through to enter. In the morning when the gray ants came forth, stirred to happy labor by the first fingers of heat, they found the soldiers there, ringed about the entrances, their skulls pressing to the sand, their bodies weighted with dew.

For days and days the soldiers stood that way. Not one was touched by the gray ants, or fed, and they never moved. And when their golden shells grew light, these were lifted, these were blown one by one by a wind down the slope, and tumbled across the clearing, and dispersed at the edge of the city, among the chaff and husks.

Thus this history is ended.

Invocation

Now I know what it is to be
like the butcher or the hardware man
with my fingers in blood or the narrow
mineral, the world gone solid overnight,
practical, a practical misery, a pair
of coins on my eyes, my pockets nestsful
of canceled tickets. Does that sound
like me? I beg You mercy, mercy,
You of the long black hair and the winter
skin. I have served Thee. This
I wear under my jacket now is no
hunchback's hump, but a blotch of shriveled
wings. Come down from the forthright
northern country. Teach me the true,
the harsh necessity. Strip me of error.
Widen my eyes. Split my back open
like a late dragonfly in summer thunder
uncrinkling on the marshgrass of everyday
surprise. I labor now, here.

—A wind

blows. Dark leaves fly up,
lessening the sun. The room grows cold.
Ah!

Judge me in Your severity.